F is for First Words

F is for First Words
Published by Kinkajou

Reproduced courtesy of Yellow House Art Licensing
www.yellowhouseartlicensing.com

A catalogue record for this book is available from the British Library

FSC
www.fsc.org
MIX
Paper from
responsible sources
FSC® C104723

Kinkajou is an imprint of Frances Lincoln Limited
74–77 White Lion Street
London N1 9PF
www.kinkajou.com

ISBN: 978-0-7112-3714-8

Printed in China

F is for First Words

A Modern Parent's Journal

For their funniest phrases
and most embarrassing moments